THE OIL LAMP

Ogaga Ifowodo

Africa World Press, Inc.

P.O. Box 1892
Trenton, NJ 08607

P.O. Box 48
Asmara, ERITREA

Africa World Press, Inc.

Cover Design: Olu Oguibe
Cover photo courtesy of Ed Kashi. Reproduced by permission.
Book Design by Roger Dormann

Library of Congress Cataloging-in-Publication Data

Ifowodo, Ogaga.
The oil lamp : (poems) / by Ogaga Ifowodo.
p. cm.
ISBN 1-59221-359-6 (hardcover) -- ISBN 1-59221-360-X (pbk.)
1. Nigeria--Poetry. I. Title.

PR9387.9.I315O37 2005
821'.914--dc22

2005000667

I saw so many flocks of naked souls,
all weeping miserably, and it seemed
that they were ruled by different decrees. …
Above that plain of sand, distended flakes
of fire showered down …
The dance of wretched hands was never done;
now here, now there, they tried to beat aside
the fresh flames as they fell.

—Dante, *Inferno*

Numbers, too, have significance: … 1001, the number of night, of magic, of alternative realities—a number beloved of poets and detested by politicians, for whom all alternative versions of the world are threats …

—Salman Rushdie, *Midnight's Children*

To:

The thousand-and-one
gone in the struggle
for a livable
Niger Delta,
a just Nigeria.

CONTENTS

ACKNOWLEDGEMENTS

The sequence of poems that forms *The Oil Lamp* was written midway into the Master of Fine Art programme which I began in the autumn of 2001 at Cornell. I wrote "The Agonist (for Ken Saro-Wiwa & the Ogoni 8)" in the autumn of 2000 while participating in that year's Iowa International Writing Programme as part of a collection which I would later abandon upon an irresistible impulse to do a one-poem book on the Niger Delta. But even the draft of "The Agonist," the only poem I have taken out of what will now be a fourth collection for its obvious blood ties to this book, benefited immensely, as the five poems of *The Oil Lamp*, from peerless readings and criticism at the weekly writing workshops. I must begin, therefore, by saying how lucky I am to have come to Cornell when Ken McClane, Alice Fulton, Phyllis Janowitz and Deborah Tall, all accomplished poets, led the workshops; to have McClane (chair), and Alice Fulton and Roger Gilbert, as ardent members of my thesis committee; and Reesa Grushka, Sean Serrel, Pauls Toutonghi, Toshiaki Komura, Emily Rosko, Chanda Amarylis Wakefield, August Smith, Ann Buechner, Theo Hummer, Cathleen Drake, Charity Ketz and Jose Beduya, as unstinting, perceptive and inspirational colleagues.

Immense gratitude to Biodun Jeyifo (BJ) whose support and encouragement dating back to 1987 when I published my first magazine poem, and at every step of the way thirteen years later, helped to smooth my road to Cornell, and also for his avuncular presence which made Ithaca even more welcoming than its famous winters had promised; to Akin Adesokan, friend and colleague who, learning from the fate of an earlier journey taken together, this time wisely arrived at Cornell ahead of me.

Much love and grateful thanks to Oke and David for a sense of family so far from home, and for making me a godfather for the first time; to Emenike and Chinyere, for the four months in Lagos before returning to school (rather late!) and, also, for making me a godfather the second time.

Lastly, I would like to thank the editors of *The Massachusetts Review* where "The Agonist (for Ken Saro-Wiwa & the Ogoni 8)" first appeared.

A Waterscape

Hung above water, hands in the air,
whited tongues and breathing fibrous hair:
roots, white mangrove roots.

Blacker than pear, deeper than soot,
massive ink-well, silent and mute:
water, black water.

Floating hats of lily, yellow plume,
plankton and shrimp, egg-and-fish in bloom:
lakes, ancestral lakes.

Rich mud of eels, water-holes of crab,
sink-place for fisher of dig-and-grab:
bog, mudskippers' bog.

And in the mangrove waters, where tides
free the creeks of weeds, fishermen glide
home to the first meal.

Part I
Jese

I

It was the fourteenth month of the fuel crunch
and stoves cooked cobwebs in cold corners.
Dreading the spirits that live in trees,

they would not break green twigs to make a meal,
till the fuel crunch compelled choice between
tree and human, today and tomorrow.

The forest quivered as trunk after trunk snapped,
and a nameless rage wagged green-fingered
branches in the air as they fell to the hungry axe.

They smelt edible death in food cooked
with logs still so alive they hissed,
then puffed out clouds of wet smoke so bitter

the women wept into their pots.
In the fourteenth month of the fuel crunch,
with oil lamps dry and dusty, nightfall

wrapped their village in a veil of ink.
They turned to candles till their need made wax gold,
forcing them to roost earlier than their hens

on moonless nights when fireflies mocked
the dimmed promise of *eletiriki*.

II

Electric light. Electric for short,
or eletiriki, when conducted
through the cables of their simple speech.

Promises made by a hard-hatted
minister at the tape-cutting for the first
well withered with the drilling tree.

When the tree glowed in the dazzle
of lighted stockades—halogen-eyed Cyclops
guarding the well—they could touch the day

shaped by a minister's words when their oil lamps
should sputter and die at the flick of a switch.
The dream of eletiriki burned bright

for forty years, powered by a plant,
till the tree drilled its last barrel.
The electric Cyclops blinked, moved

to another well in another place
to guard a fresh promise of light.
Now the rusted sinews of the tree,

heaped on the slick-crusted site of the well,
glower at the sky, a promise in rust-flakes.

III

This was how the damage was done,
with old pipes corroded and cracked
by the heat of their burden –

petrol and paraffin piped away
from rotting dugouts and thatched huts
          to float ships and fly planes,

          to feed factories and the chain of ease
          to heat stoves and save the trees
          to light house and street at break of night,

          to make fortunes for faceless traders
in markets without stalls or hand-made goods.
A sickened earth rusted the pipes

and threw up the lie encased in hollow metal.
Four boys chasing rodents for the day's meal –
while their mates in cities where the pipes end

learnt their letters in song and rhyme – were first
to find the fountain. The mist of gushing oil
blinded them long before the blaze. Their screams

summoned the village for the hot shower,
the ritual bath before sacrifice.

tale of two cities scene?

IV

They followed the rodent hunters to the heart
of the fountain. In a moment
the fear sprayed on their heads, chilling their bones

like a viper's mist, fled, broke their grim mouths
into smiles. Without word or sign,
they hurried home to fetch pails and kegs,

cups and funnels. It was the fourteenth month
of the fuel crunch, the stumps of felled trees
sprouting new life, the village still.

The broken pipes, like the mouth of a river,
carved two brooks of kerosene and petrol.
And like that Gaulish crowd, crazed by cracked

casks of wine on a cobbled street,
vampiric
a siphoning circus danced to the wild
music of deprivation in the low growth,

and they fought for elbow room
to fill their bowls and kegs
with the spilled oil of their land

near a drilled-dry well, its drilling tree
the lurking brown ghost of eletiriki.

V

And soon, stoves and lamps burned again.
A roadside oil trade boomed, brought life
back to the stilled village, sparked the trek

to a visible oil market where dealers
sold in kegs and bottles for naira,
not in barrels at trade floors for dollars.

The news came on the twelfth night:
“A breach in a refined products pipeline
in Jese, Delta State, has led to a scramble

by villagers for kerosene and petrol.
While government regrets the hardship
caused by the current fuel crisis,

now in its second year, it wishes to warn
that the breach poses serious danger to life
and property and to advise a stop to the scramble.”

A rumour, said the wild music of deprivation,
deaf to words unable to light stoves and lamps.
The scramble went on, till the riot police came

and shooting to disperse the frenzied crowd
blazed the fiery trail of law and order.

VI

That was Odiri's tale of the cause of the fire
moaned from a bed in the local clinic,
whose calico sheets, gummed to her bum

and back, were the graft for slipped-off skin.
She had fallen face-up, hands in front to reach
for her daughter as the flames engulfed her.

A full keg of kerosene on her head,
she had stepped out of the pool, now ankle high,
to wait till her daughter filled a buffer keg

when she saw the raised arms and guns.
The crack of trigger on hammer, her daughter's
cries, and the shrieks of the scavenging crowd

became a deafening *whoooosh!* As sheets of fire,
like flags of hell in gusty breeze, enwrapped
arms flung in fright at the surprised air, cumuli of smoke

smothered the last tremors, the sizzles of body
fat melting to add oil to oil, the crackle
of bones bursting alight, the gurgle

in her throat. And she sank into a pit, burned
till she woke in a bed gummed to her back.

VII

But what can we trust she saw? remembered?
Her daughter lighting up the sky
before a cloud swallowed her? The finger

at the trigger? The keg falling from her head,
its spilled contents burning a path to her feet?
Hear another tale of how the fire started:

a bus driver, dizzy with the joy
of a week's hoard of petrol, struck
a reckless match for the celebration

cigarette – his last visit to a filling station
too far back to recall the "No Smoking"
caution. Or the cause blamed on the season:

a brush fire, set by a slash-and-burn farmer,
threw sparks carried by the harmattan wind
to the heady fountain. And yet another:

An old woman, too frail for the daytime scuffle,
had sought her chance by night. An oil lamp
in a grandson's hand, she was filling

her Ovaltine can when a growl in the bush
startled the boy who dropped the lamp in the pool.

VIII

And the smoke rose mournfully from the ground,
from the sizzle of mixed oils licked
by fiery tongues from each drying bone

(cracked alight unseen to the watering eye).
The smoke rose cloudily from the ground,
its freight of ashes weightier than the burning bodies.

In the widening bowl, blackening the clay,
a burning bush blazed out of the book of terror
burning brighter night and day with every

gnash of teeth, withered wail and cindered word.
The smoke rose heavily from the ground
bearing to an implacable god its meal:

a burnt offering of its worshippers –
not communion food, not sirloin or
tenderloin or calcium-bone, but the scented air

rising from the ashening earthen censer.
The smoke curled lugubriously from the ground
twirled around a stairway of despair

on which prayer and pity lost their step,
and reclaimed by the fire, lost all hope.

IX

The smoke bore food to a severe god,
but to a village sent to sleep by hunger,
a sign of the end of time. They wakened

from their nightmares to the greetings of fire
shrieked across dismal doorways by a child
demented by the deafening *whooosh!* blinded

by the dazzle of her mother's hair glowing
for a maddening moment like filaments of gold.
Led by the venomous scent of charring bone,

the dripping and drying fat of breasts and buttocks
spiced by the aromatic thyme of the shrivelling
shrubbery, they rushed to the edges of the blaze

but checked by the furious fence twirled by the smoke
round its infernal altar, the men's eyes
reddened, then moistened, as they ran for water;

the women broke out of their breast-beating fear
quickly enough to clutch at sand and stones
to throw in handfuls at the furnace.

But all was fuel to the consuming fire,
bones and flesh as stones and sand and the thrown water.

X

They came swiftly to the wreck, the prey birds,
circling the rising and spreading smoke,
praying for good game as they hunted on the wing.

They darkened further the sky, their wings
stretched tip to tip like a giant tent.
Their laser vision pinpointed the rabbit

scurrying away from its hole, the leaping frog,
the dazed rodent surprised by the flames;
their vision mocked the frantic crowd.

Atop the yellowing branches of rubber trees
haemorrhaging fortunes for distant lands,
vultures held their perch, their downward-hooked heads

questioning nothing but a spoiling of their feast
by the flames set on cackling till the last cinder;
but kings of carrion wisdom, they knew their open

banquet hall, like a battlefield, marked
calamity with enough bodies of the slain,
could never fail their patience or appetite.

The hopes of preying birds rose with the smoke
as dry throats gave their last breath to the air.

XI

The fire uncoiled like an infinite
cobra, stretched to the farthest edges
of a land marked by oil for double torment.

And the fields of crops, snatched from water
by the hands of simple farmers, screamed:

It's midseason! We are not ripe!
Do not reap us! Do not cook us!

The creeks and ponds, soon to boil dry,
joined the fields, thinking the case
of water even clearer and cried:

Take your cooking oil away
We are no pots or cauldrons!
Can't you see here's no kitchen
And you burn your meal to ashes?

The rivers, now on fire, rushed
to the sea for a dip, floating
along the land's burning question,

unanswerable as every spot soaked the flow
and wind and water showed the fire where to go.

XII

The land burned, the trees burned, the rivers burned,
the smoke unrolled endless bolts of cloth
to wrap naked grief and shield the world

from the horrors of the flames. It was harmattan,
best for bonfires and spreading with the wind
scorched-earth policies framed in secret rooms

beyond the sea. The reigning rogue, sprung
from a gun's barrel or broken ballot box,
sped through the traffic-cleared street, through unpaved

paths – throwing dust in prying eyes – to the State House;
there he stamped and sealed the deed for immediate
execution, and in council with his henchmen,

unveiled the many plans for ridding
the land of its human blight and digging
for the liquid gold beneath their feet.

This was the peace plan: death by hunger or fire.
It was fire for Jese, ashes and scars for all
but the head of state who wiped his face and said:

> *I came to see the damage you have done*
> *and the roast dinner for me and my guests.*

XIII

A harmattan bush, doused by an oil fountain.
After the deafening *whoooosh!* some ran for creeks
and rivers, some jumped in water-wells,

some rolled on the ground, and some beat themselves
or were beaten with broken branches.
But the fire raced ahead of many,

and going where it wished, raged far from firemen,
far from access roads, far from where it mattered,
for nights and days till it burnt itself out

under a drizzle, with nothing left to burn,
when what was left was what would not burn.
Charred remains, whole enough to count,

bloated bodies fished from creeks, wells and rivers,
totalled a thousand, the record-keepers said –
far from where stubborn bones queried the count.

Will the government aid the victims of Jese?
The head-of-state, visiting the village,
and pained to his soul, lowered his head,

then steadied his nerves: No, he said,
we must not encourage thieves and saboteurs.

this word.. political weight & connotation

XIV

And this the head-of-state's finding, in a telecast
relayed by radio, carried by the papers:
a dangerous band of youths sworn to sabotage

for redress of perceived wrongs,
had taken to breaching pipelines
(among other dastardly acts)

across the length and breadth
of the Delta, in the hope of gaining
the world's attention and embarrassing

their country and government,
as they did three years earlier by murdering
four elders opposed to their crimes.

Timing their latest act for the worst moment
of the current crisis, they caused the breach
and the scramble that led to the fire.

For the avoidance of doubt, government
wishes to make clear that the police
arrived too late to stop the fire

clearly lit as they landed on the scene
by youths detailed for the purpose.

poetic voice carried by papers

XV

Madam Edoja, ninety years of age,
fifty years a widow since her husband
fell off a rig and drowned at sea,

sat in a makeshift tent, called for water
to quench the fire still raging in her throat
and broke ninety days of silence with a song:

> Oil is my curse, oil is our doom.
> *Where is my husband, where my only love?*
> *At the bottom of the sea, the bottom of the sea.*
>
> Oil is my curse, oil is our doom.
> *Where is the fish for palm-oil soup?*
> *Dead in the creeks, dead in the lakes.*
>
> *Oh mate, do you have a cup of garri*
> *to lend me for the children's sake?*
> *Not even a cup, not even a handful!*
>
> *The fields are tarred where cassava once grew,*
> *you know the fields are tarred and harder*
> *than a shell, too hard for our hoes.*
>
> Oil is my curse, oil is my doom.
> *Where are my children? Where is my husband?*
> *Ashes and bones. Ashes and bones.*

Part II
Odi

XV1

A battalion of justice scorched its path
to Odi, came to solve by war
a case of homicide: five cops and four

soldiers sent to break a youth revolt
lay dead in the dark labyrinth of the delta,
engorging sharks or crocodiles, or growing rank

with slick-spiked creek water. And the president,
ex-commando, false-star general,
summoned the governor of the province

for his orders: "By noon tomorrow, find
the murderers or prepare the grounds for my men."
And the governor: "Sir, for thirty days

I have searched every house twice night and day;
I have sat men and women, older
than my grandfather under sun and rain;

I have let children cry unfed till they slept;
I have combed every tree's head, burnt every
fishhut, rowed all the creeks, and not found them,

nor found anyone, young or old, that knew them.
I need no grace. Come, Sir, at once for the arrest."

XVII

The first grenade, lobbed by a hand
too eager for live cremations, landed
on the roof of the village school.

The fire and the alarm started there
with the wiping out of the house of learning.
They had come to perfect what rain and wind

began weeks before by stripping the mud-
walled classroom blocks of their thatch roofs.
In the thick of the season's night-and-day

downpours, the walls washed down to hardwood
posts and bamboo grids were at home with defeat.
Hearing no shrieks, the sort his well-trained soldier's

ears knew as the terror of a shell-shattered
night just before dawn, he steadied his hand
for the second lob, this time in line with the rest

of the troops. He heard then a demented
dog's barking and the bleating of goats,
the cackle of chickens, then the screams

and the panicked dash for the bush—from lighted
homes to safety in the formless side of the night.

XVIII

Dawn bared their states of undress, mocked
the women's peasant propriety
as homes crumbled and the bush waved in vain

its green scarves for peace. They huddled under trees
and counted a bomb when the ground shook, till
it rumbled as if the god of thunder

had changed his throne. Fear stilled the ungovern-
able mouths of babies strapped to backs with
bedspreads grabbed by instinct at the moment of flight.

Crickets, outshouted, scurried
in dazed circles around children too stunned
to stretch out a hand, until hunger matched fear

and the men, far from yam or fish, turned insect
hunters, wild root diggers. Banished
from fire by fire, they ate their food fresh.

It was dark when they fled their beds,
dark again when they knelt in silence,
prayed the invaders to accept victory and go home,

but heard the ground tremble, the sky rumble,
and the trees wave again in vain.

XIX

The governor headed for his waiting jet
hastening to the head-of-state's summons,
his sirens and outriders cutting

the fear-thickened air like shrapnel.
Odi, far from gubernatorial lodges
and bomb-proof bunkers, heard the echo

of his flight. Pa Piriye, born eighteen years
before the British punitive expedition
to Benin, shook woefully his head,

revived his tales of 1897
and drove the cautious to their bundles, the trek
to outlying towns and villages, fishhuts and dugouts.

It was the hopeful few, fooled by their longing
for the peace of home and settled soil,
that beat a frenzied path to the bush

as the roof of the village school yawned,
swallowed a grenade and forked the night
into wild branches of fire. With each blast,

each *booom!* magnified by the silence of their abandoned
homes, they clutched at trembling twigs for a shred of hope.

XX

They heard a thud in a clump of bamboo,
then the tea-black water of the lake
they had drunk for a night and a day exploded.

They scattered with the muddy splash
deeper into the bush. Shell-shocked, babies
and children smothered the instinct to cry

and clammed to backs and shoulders and the held-
out hand, brave as their parents clinging
to the hope of return to their homes cross-

haired by the demolition man, as they sought
cover under leaves in a shuddering forest.
The air shrieked behind them and the walnut tree,

a moment ago their home, cleaved
into two by another bomb,
crashed, lashing a mother and child

at the backline of flight. And now
the children bawled, and their parents
finding words for the terror cried:

We're dead! We're dead!
Save us, O God!

XXI

It proved a sign of capitulation
enough for a moment's truce: the crazed dog,
silent as a bone, skin drawn tighter

over its ribs than a drum of war,
zigzagged to the fish-market and died.
The detective soldiers knew then that all

but the murderers, crouched in ambush
behind off-hinge doors, armed and ready
for battle, had fled. It was time

for the house-to-house search
to fish them out. In the high noon
hazed by the dust and smoke

of their bombs, in the silence
heavier than a ghost-town's,
they kicked in doors, but remembering

the mission, the glory
of a parade with living trophies,
duly cautioned at every door:

This is the army! You cannot win!
Come out with your hands above your heads!

XXII

Noontide breeze, mordant with the smell
of justice, blew into deserted homes
through blown-out windows, broken walls, fallen

roofs, sent the echo of their warning
where the enemy might hear it and surrender.
Still, they heard only their boots on doors,

the crashing walls and rafters
which, shaken loose, collapsed at their feet.
But the breeze cooled the sweat of battle

on their skin, dried their starched fatigues
to knife-edge sharpness, envigoured
the toughness of the bombing phase.

And they shot grenades into houses
suspiciously unmarked, dropped
on bellies, machine guns on the ready,

to await the squealing caved-in faces of fear
and surrender. Still, they heard only
their thumping boots, the tumbling-in

of roofs, and walls crumbling
before the charge at the blasted door.

XXIII

There were no surrenders. In the house-to-
house search, they saw, in a cement-plastered
mudhut, the army combat kit: fatigues, olive wide

buckle belt hanging from a wall, dusty boots
and helmet, stripped, no doubt, from a murdered
soldier. Shielded from three quick bombs

by avocado trees and a taller house,
the cement-plastered mudhut
escaped the suspicion-grenades

when a pear tree fell on it. The sight
of the combat kit fired their *esprit de corps*
to battle frenzy, and raging out of the hut,

they emptied their rifles on the walls,
on the wing of the roof unbroken
by the fallen tree, shouting now

no police cautions, but war cries:
Come out cowards, bloody bastards!
So you ambush four soldiers, kill them

and think you're brave. Come out!
Show us now how many more you can kill!

XXIV

What they had not seen was the body
of Sergeant Tobi, alias One Nigeria,
crushed to death by the falling tree.

Paralysed by a spinal-cord wound
in the Biafran war, he lay face-up,
no longer begging God for his death

as he had done for thirty years. Glad
to hear the sound of bombs, he'd scorned
flight, the bonds of love, saying: "One war spared

only my breath, froze me to a bed.
Let this mark my end." And he willed
the trunk of the tree on his head,

the slicing edge of a zinc sheet on his throat.
And now, demented by a comrade's
disembodied kit, they no longer cared

to kick down doors, but threw the suspicion-
grenade at every house with its roof aloft,
the fierce noonlight too hazed by their smoky

rage to show them how faded the uniform was,
how old and dusty the boots and helmet.

XXV

A dead soldier, but no soldier-killer.
At the fishmarket, they grabbed the dead dog,
split it open, and dipping finger,

like brush in paint, wrote
on standing doors and walls
the lethal terms of truce:

THIS IS THE END OF ODI
THIS IS WHAT WE DO TO COWARDS
THIS IS JUST A WARNING

NEXT TIME YOU SEE SOJA YOU GO RUN!
NEXT TIME WE WILL SHOW NO MERCY
NEXT TIME FOR ONE SOJA YOU WILL ALL DIE!

The last clause of the truce was barely legible,
the dog's blood running out on them, but they knew
what was left unsaid spoke even louder

from heaps of rubble and the mordant air.
But back in their armoured carriers, returning
with no suspect in their net, were civil

enough to tell a fisherman too long away at sea,
"You have no home anymore. Go back to sea!"

XXVI

The noise of ordnance was dead, so was Odi.
They saw the headlines in nearby towns and villages,
heard the news spread by word of mouth in the bush:

"Odi flattened, pays the heaviest price yet."
"There's no place called Odi anymore, says soldier."
"We'll protect our oil wealth at any cost, says President."

They returned with hands above their heads,
bewailing their lost homes, cursing
what fate buried oil in their patch of earth.

And Pa Piriye, hair and beard all white,
saw the ruins of his house, the dog's blood sign
NEXT TIME YOU SEE SOLDIER YOU WILL RUN!

scrawled in vermilion scorn across his door,
and he said, *I have lived too long. Today, my feet*
sink into the ground at the sight of my door.

When British soldiers looted and burned Benin,
we cursed strange men come from beyond the sea,
from the land of the dead, so evil they had no skin.

But who shall we curse now, who now is the enemy?
My eyes have seen two evils, must not see another.

XXVII

The fisherman spurned the warning.
Away for months at sea, he pined
for wife and children. The air, still thick

with a smell not of sea or shore or human place,
made him shiver like fish flung on beach, made him
cry as in a sea funeral in front of his house,

till he saw faces emerge out of the bush,
too stunned to cry, slowly begin
the digging for shirts and shoes,

pots and pans to beat back into shape,
knives and hoes and fishing nets,
and he began to dig for what he couldn't tell

till the burnt schoolbag reminded him,
and *The Fisherman's Invocation,*
the book of poems he couldn't read,

that his daughter—*where is she? where are they?*—
read to welcome him from sea, seared
his throat with a thirst for her voice. He held

the book and wept into the ashes of burnt-out things,
the bitter memory of unusable fragments.

XXVIII

Their house already flattened,
aimless flight landed the last grenade
softly yards away where the bush began.

It buried itself in the beach-sand,
like an armoured dragon's egg,
proto-smart bomb that knows, must find,

its enemy, flash *mission accomplished!*
in forked fingers of fire.
It was a simple house, just enough

for a young teacher couple and son.
Three years of exile had hidden the rubble
under lush weeds that shuddered sadly

in the evening breeze. Back to rebuild
the house, the cutting and clearing was done.
He left for the city, for builders' things still lacking;

she was to gather and burn the last heaps of rubbish;
lit, they blazed in the August sun. Her baby played
safely far from the fire, so she went for a jug

of water. Then the armoured dragon's egg, hatch-hot,
dug a grave foundation for the new house.

Part III
Ogoni

XXIX

Major Kitemo, boss of the mob,
chief pacifier
of the lower Niger's

still primitive tribes, had at last laid waste
the prickly land. And speaking to the press
about the good job he had done for

country
conscience
posterity,

showed what a half-breed the people were
to claim and fight for what they did not own,
to deny the owners what was theirs

by decrees duly made and in the books;
showed why extreme measures were called for
to teach the needed lesson, stem the tide

of defiance which, for three years,
had shut down Shell's oil wells
and slimmed the nation's purse;

showed how deficient words had proved,
how efficient persuasion by other means.

XXX

I went to their leaders—no, not the Ken Saro-Wiwas
of the foreign-sponsored MOSOP and NYCOP[1]—
I went to the women, fishermen, farmers,

and jobless youths they had brainwashed,
to bring them to reason, and I asked them,
"Do you really believe you own the oil?"

"Yes," they said, as I knew they would.
"And how did you come to own it?"
"By its being on our land," they said.

"The land is Nigeria's," I corrected them.
And then an old man, parched and cracked
far worse than any sun-sucked patch

of spill-soaked land I have seen, asked in return
"And how did Nigeria come to own the oil?"
Oh, I should have paused to give thought,

should never have presumed a hoary-headed man,
but I answered too quickly, "By its being
on her land." It was a minor slip,

a momentary lapse of no consequence
to the crack prosecutor's cast-iron case.

[1] Movement for the Survival of the Ogoni People, whose chief moving spirit was the writer and activist, Ken Saro-Wiwa, executed along with 8 other activists by the military regime of General Sani Abacha on 10 November 1995. NYCOP is the National Youth Congress of the Ogoni People.

XXXI

The old man, ready with a riposte,
was speaking again. I was losing patience,
but I have an old father, his head a hat of wool,

so I let him speak, just one more time.
And what treason! what outrage! He said:
"Can you tell me, my son, how old Nigeria is?"

I can't tell now why I was so rash,
expert that I am at squelching mischief
before it buds, but I spoke too soon:

"Born in 1914, she's seventy-nine this year," I said.
And he: "That's Lord Lugard's colony, the cartographer's
trade map for British expropriation. But I

will take your word for it, So tell me, my son,
How long do you think we have been on this land,
how long the oil, the trees, the creeks and the rivers?"

Oh, never take an old man for granted
nor the mist and webs of times past;
still it was no case for history,

nor the error more than a minor slip,
but I had seen the strength of their delusion.

XXXII

I had to regain lost ground, be interrogator
again, and steer clear of foggy waters,
so I said: "By decrees and edicts

duly made, the land is not yours
nor all that lies in it. The powers
that rule the country—your colony—

that make you citizens
of a nation, known to law
and safe from plunder,

decree the land and its wealth not yours."
It wasn't the old man again, God knows
I would not have let him; it was a woman

and I thought, What can a woman say
to loosen one rivet of the law?
And she said, in plain pidgin,

No vex o, Oga[2] *soja, but who*
or wetin make up dis Nigeria?
There were many hands now up, no doubt

with more cheek and treason,
the hard rote of lawlessness.

[2] Used often as an honorific, the nearest equivalent in standard English would be "boss." The lines may be rendered thus: "Do not be offended, officer / but who and what make up this Nigeria?"

XXXIII

I'd had enough, but now it was a child
barely through high school, in ragged
uniform. I'd noticed his fixed stare

at my crisp khakis and mirror-clean boots.
I raised my hand to say, Listen to me,
there'll be no more impudence, no more false

claims and clever arguments, but he spoke—
too calmly for a child, I must say—
and as I kept my hand up, the old man said,

"Do you fear a child's words too?"
I had to let him speak. "Excuse me, sir," he said,
"but in whose name, and by whose powers,

were the laws you cite made?" It was unreal,
an ancient, a female and a sapling,
had taken words from me! But though to a soldier

that's nothing of shame, I had to have
the last word, show an officer is brains
and brawn, as sharp in mind as his hard-pressed

pleats. I said, "So you own the oil, but what
did you do with it buried in the ground?"

XXXIV

They were rattled; no hands were up now,
so I chased the enemy home
back against a wall of his own.

It was true. What did they know of oil
other than the fruit-red extract of palm trees?
The bounty of the sea, of the creeks and rivers,

the barn-busting yield of arable land
rich in organic silt and loam
had not caused a quest for riches

hidden deep in the heart of the earth.
When they dug wells, it was for water;
They didn't have to dig too deep for the table,

didn't have to drill to the heart
or mine every vein for fossil ooze,
until the colonial find in '58

at Oloibiri—not even in their land!
But they found their tongue once more,
in a former teacher, the plucky child's father:

"But for the theft by law, we would in time
have seismographed and drilled, or hired Shell."

XXXV

There was nothing for it: words had failed.
No child, man or woman could be swayed;
they had the script in their heads,

answers for every question. I
had now to follow my own script,
outlined in my Memo for Peace

to the Commander-in-Chief.
First, cure them of the lies
drilled into their bones by rabble-rousers;

if that failed, set them against themselves,
cause feuds with neighbours,
and if still true to the rote, still starving

the treasury of petro-dollars, launch
the last plan: Wasting Operations,
group infiltration, mass deportations.

"Can you do it, can you secure the target?"
the C-in-C wished to know. "Sir," I said,
"I have the best skills your army can give,

I have excess of zeal. What is more, I know
two hundred and twenty-one ways to kill a man."

XXXVI

I had used two centuries of killing skills,
yet they clung to their claim.
There were, of course, some gains: only

the cause-crazed, craving martyrdom,
dared come to rallies or picket oil wells.
But I knew I was far from winning

when one said at gunpoint,
mouth and nose frothing blood,
"If I starve to death on a Shell-shocked

bog, or fall off a deep-sea rig and drown,
taking my tears like coal to Newcastle,
I will have died as I lived—to no end.

But if Major Kill-Them-All (yes,
that's what they had begun to call me)
shot or tortured me to death

for linking hands with my brothers
to stop the drilling of another barrel
then my death might dig deeper into the land

the anger that chokes me when I sleep,
make me a landmine to trampling boots."

XXXVII

Far from winning, the C-in-C's trust waning,
I had to go for the last plan, secure the target.
But I lacked a pretext, the aggressive

act of folly gladly embraced. I was charged
to go shooting from the hip, but I'd had
truly bad press: none of you here now helped

my cause an inch. You made a monster of me,
accepting like holy writ every word Ken spoke;
the playwright[3] and poet, he made plain words

cry false wrongs on your desks till you reached out
a hand to console him, picked your pens for the scoop,
and I could never match him word-for-word,

if I couldn't have the last word
with children, women and old men.
I was close to despair, ready

to give you the prize headline, shoot myself
in the foot. Then they sprung the trap! I
had set it with the perfect bait, prepared

with inhuman patience. It was time,
and I flung my arms in the air.

[3] Ken Saro-Wiwa, the moving spirit and spokesman of MOSOP, was a poet, novelist and dramatist. Until 1993 when his minority and environmental rights activism overshadowed his reputation as a writer, including being president of the Association of Nigerian Authors, he was, in fact, better known for his highly successful network TV drama series, *Basi & Company*.

XXXVIII

I preferred the nights when oil lamps twinkled
over the evening tide catch in wet nets,
fish-women smelling of *eau de poisson*

and buyers bent like shrimps over trays and mats,
haggling over prices without a care. We'd
surround the town but keep the roads clear.

At my word, big guns would go off
and at first, the fish-market, always
a hubbub equal to the sea's roar,

would be dead-still, and you could hear
a lamp, its oil drying, splutter its rage,
or the chink of change dropped by shocked hands.

We paused for the awe to revive them,
till we saw them fling away the fish
as if they were marine bombs! We sustained

fire then till all the lamps gasped and surrendered
to night, till only the light of our fire streaked
in the bloated darkness as houses quenched

their lamps to hide their fear, and their occupants
fled to the bush through the paths of flight I'd kept open.

XXXIX

Major Kill-Them-All. At first I was mad
at the brave wretch. Soldier or not, it wounded
my Christian heart. I yelled at him:

"It's Major Kitemo, understand? you
bloody Good-for-Nothing! No one fools
with my name, you hear?" Then I was glad

to know they'd killed four men, calling
them traitors, vultures gorging on kinsmen's
corpses. Yes, I'd set the trap, unspooling

threads of suspicion, spinning webs
around them with words that failed
at town meetings, grown forceful with bribes

and slander. Multiple murders: I had now
the aggressive act of folly, so I said: "Kill-
Them-All, not so? Well, you'd better run! I

will wipe out every damn one of you, if I must."
Guns and grenades yelled my new name for fifteen days.
I drove them all into the bush, sent them rowing

into the creeks with fireflies as their light. Then we dug
in to hold the town, shooting to keep them in the bush.

XL

Shooting and bombing to keep them in the bush
we were running out of ammo by the tenth day,
but Shell shipped in caseloads of what we lacked.

Fifteen nights and days in swamps and creeks
broke them. First, they pushed out two little girls,
who kept running back, scared to death. Then, a boy

and a girl. As the matinée grenades went off,
they fainted. I'd waited for the surrender;
we took them in and kept shelling. I wanted

the smart-ass quartet: the old man, the schoolboy
and his father, the woman. I didn't have to wait long.
They came out among a crowd and fell on their knees:

Please, please, we will do what you say, anything
you want. But stop the shelling. Please! Please!
"What about your oil, you don't want it anymore?"

Three have died of snakebites, four of malaria.
Two women have given birth under trees. Five elders' hearts
expired with the last bomb. Our stomachs are raw with roots.

Let us live. Please! Please! I let them live,
took prisoners, and brightened my epaulettes.

Part IV
The Pipes War

XLI

They hanged nine
for murders pre-planned
and Colonel Kitemo

had, at last, his last word.
The troubled peace of surrender
churned stomachs, threw up

the bile of raw-root meals
eaten in the bush, renewed the taste
of uncontainable grief

for all too weak to be right,
too few for a moment's doubt
in the mind of the well-paid hand,

money-on-the-barrel to the oil cartel
for containment strategies
when the natives get restive.

"After fifteen nights and days in the bush,
they came to me, begging, *Let us live. Please! Please!*
Anything to stop the bombing. Please! Please!"

That was the swashbuckler's boast in barrack pitch,
hear it from the bureaucrat's well-oiled tongue:

XLII

Can anyone think of the Niger Delta
and not feel an ache in his heart?
So inhospitable, it is like all terrains

in the world where oil might be found: under
seas, desert dunes, snow-capped wilds, malarial
swamps. As if He who desolated

those places thought it too cruel to plant
humans in some of them without recompense;
still I think He erred to give in remorse

to so few what must belong to all.
But a good man's conscience
will sting him like bees to see how abject

they are that live amidst such wealth in our
land; to hear them bewail the dissipation
of their share of earth's bounty, the devastation

that pours oil on rivers to float fish
lure the flamingo to a lethal meal
and quill the secretary bird's death on sludge;

that irrigates lowland crops to rot their roots,
and wells resentment like ocean tides above their heads.

XLIII

I would be first to plead their case, and say,
Pamper the goose that lays the golden eggs!
But so difficult is the land, so absurd

their claim for redress, that it should empty
the coffers and deny the nation's engine
its lubricant. Rust would follow; there'd be an end

to motion and a nation to call our own.
But though resentment swirls and eddies
in every house and raft in the Delta,

the demographics of their grief makes it easy
to contain, blunts the sharpest arrow
that may fly from any fray they are forced to start.

The wealth of nations, by fair distribution,
makes no fortunes. And Nature, unjust
sharer of its gifts, favours the stronger arm.

Unable to threaten
the settled peace
of the realm

there's nothing to fear; we can let them weep
rivers of blood till despair drives them to sleep or folly.

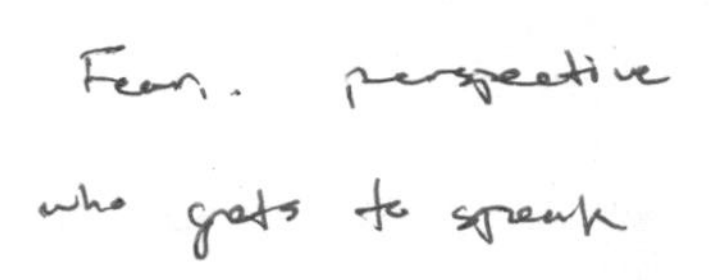

XLIV

Such folly
as Major Kitemo's pretext in Ogoni,
as flattened a town for a felony,

as burned one thousand officially dead,
as turned a scrapping for used pipes
—so rusted Shell could dig them up!—

into a war for territory
between Oleh and Olomoro:
with oil wells and pipelines, without piped water,

(but also without tribal feuds
over ancestral lands or lakes);
they had shared peace and poverty

till pipes too old for hot crude
called for heated blood in their hollows.
Oh, do not ask history's questions,

know only that claims clashed over rust,
a youth from Oleh died, and Olomoro's
equalled the spillage, and guns and matchets

leapt into hordes of hands, and there was a pretext
to shoot and burn, and drive more into the bush.

XLV

They scrap for a living
where the land's promise was boundless ease.
The fisherman throws his net, rejoices

for a single meal's catch, as trawlers
haul in schools of fish. Tankers,
whose docking and leaving make his canoe

rock to the wild tune of their wakes, sail away
with Bonny Light crude. And far
from the lighted Jetty, he paddles home

by the flame of Iron-Dragon—
the gas-flaring stack whose awful mouth spits fire
without cease near his village. Born before

the first built by Shell, he too had cursed
the dragon, called it Hell's Gorge,
sure to retch on every head afflictions and deaths

sucked from the depths of the earth;
till the women found its oven heat perfect
for drying tapioca. Till he—in the absence

of eletiriki—renamed the red tongues snarling
at the inky skies, Oil Lamps of the Delta.

Part V
Cesspit of the Niger Area

XLVI

What tears have not been shed
cannot be shed now,
what grief still unprinted

has no tree to pulp
its words that burn the tongue,
that choke the windpipe.

Broken verses, wept
far from the hidden pit,
where they flung the famous nine,

after the under-
taker's conjuration acid
(which, as we heard,

was to erase their bones,
wipe out every trace
of a deed too foul

to stay under the ground)
have dinned the air, etched
the proof on every soil.

But the many scars that itch and wounds that bleed
far from the eyes of the world beg a few more songs.

XLVII

Such as this I heard a mother sing:
The child was down with a fever
so we boiled herbs and barks for him,
still the heat rose higher and higher

till you could roast yam by his side,
so high I feared he would die.
But there's no doctor in Asaba-Ase,
no clinic in a hundred miles,

and no motorway to where he aches.
So I said to his father,
"Quick! quick! we must go to Port Harcourt,
and he said, "Dear wife, it's midnight!

Tomorrow at crack of dawn
I will go by speedboat. The times
are past, my dear, when we sang:

If you must go to Port Harcourt
and be there before it's dark,
take enough garri *and smoked fish*

say a prayer to Mamiwata[4]
and paddle off in the dead of night.

[4] Mermaid, believed to have magical powers.

XLVIII

Wonodi's wife's waters broke too soon
now sighs have replaced our song,
Wonodi's wife's womb is too fertile
now worry stiffens our smiles,

for she has given birth to five
a month and a half before her time
and old Tobrise the midwife
has only pots and pans and hot water.

Quick! quick! we must hurry to Warri!
where they say there's a machine
to save the ones that come too soon,
quick, quick, pull out canoes and paddles.

And you ask: Did life reward the journeys?
Did your man reach Port Harcourt by dusk
Is the ailing child back in your bosom?

Oh you ask: Did they make it to Warri
Did Olokun[5] calm the waters,
and the machine quicken them for her arms?

I will not answer! I will not answer!
Look at my arms! Go to her house!

[5] God of the sea.

XLIX

And this from a man with a grudge in Warri:
The whole town in darkness
because Never Expect Power Always[6]
is working hard for its name.

First, there was light every other day,
then every two days, then four, then …
Forty-five days! Can't sleep at night—
without the fan to stun mosquitoes.

See where I live—a shack in the swamp!
But light shines on the oil staff estates—
well-drained and paved and mosquito-proof.
Went past one today as I tramped for work,

and seeing those carpet-lawns, the quiet
order of the place, shamed me to the bone;
didn't want to go home then, I felt like a sewer rat!

That's when I said, "Listen, Solomon,
you're nobody's fool. Be wise! Good job,
fine house, sleek car and beautiful woman

are for Solo too. That's your money, man!
And I'm going to live even if I die first.

[6] As Nigeria's state-owned energy monopoly, the National Electric Power Authority (NEPA), is popularly called due to its staggering inefficiency.

L

And now with naked malice, I must deny
Major Kitemo (and his ilk) the last word,
give it to his nemesis, the schoolboy,

now a sophomore at law, unaware
what paths to even sharper perception
the gods, offended by bombs, prepare

for his itching feet as he writes under a tree
—and I copy—the words of the shaping
poet, peeling the scabs to regrow the skin:

The Niger flows down to us the pus of the land,
East and West of the putrid heart, two valves
pump dead blood into our open veins. And we

are silted gutters, swamp and swampdwellers.
The Niger flows down to us its floodwaters,
swells our rivers with the dread tributes

of seasonal carnage washed in from the fields.
And we stay afloat by treading tears, reclaiming
footholds with the humus of hate and envy.

And when they rise to spit on our heads the rinse-water
of their early morning mouths, I remember the dew,
the one thousand and one gone, and what will remain true.

The Agonist

(for Ken Saro-*Wiwa* & the Ogoni 8)

1 Let Us Pretend We Can Write It

Let us pretend we can write it, using
words that fled with the air from the tightening
noose to maintain their ground, words that floated
belly-up in the creek, their eyes coated

with the ash of the fire beneath. Let us
plait to the hair the maddened mourner plucked
from her head, the word that's cry and loss and curse
and ask forgiveness for those that mocked.

But where is the word and where is the hand
to match the heart that bleeds alone? Don't ask!
Pray only to trace the silence and the scream

and fix to its spot of earth
(which the murderer denies the martyr)
the echo with which our cry hallows their death.

2 Memory was His Saviour and His Death

Memory was his saviour. And his death!
He remembered the swamps and the rivers,
the fish shivering in a choked net,
the colony of creeks and mudskippers

founded by retreating tides. And the farms
swollen with roots and bulbs. He remembered
a bounty whose splendour wrote psalms
chanted by the peasant to winds and birds.

Memory was his saviour and his death.

He had known the floods, the tides and the waves
that softened the land and brought the fish home;
at one with nature's lore, they left no graves.

He came to know the black springs of the fuel oil
spewing liquid fire from iron pythons
coiled like rigs of death round their love and toil;

he came to know cities floated on the oil
plundered from the land under his feet, where
councils held in big halls to share the spoils

and memory became his saviour from death

when the housewife stood aghast by her plot
of cassava and herbs swallowed by slick

when trees, fish and animals in mourning
surrendered to acid rain and gas poison

when the canoe paddling children to school
capsized far from bridge or motorway

when the army invaded the village
shooting bombing burning raping laughing!

when the commander of the mob boasted
two hundred and twenty-one ways of killing,

memory became his saviour from the death
when he bore witness to the rape and the shame!

3 Hurry Them Down into the Grave

Hurry him down, hurry them down into the grave,
hurry them down before their bones nail my guilt.
Now my eyes are redder than the blood I have spilled
and my vision no further than my gilded chair
recedes into my head to blaze forth my fear,
hurry him down, hurry them down into the grave.

Hurry! hurry! time marches against me swifter
than the horse. Before their blood cools, warned the witches,
they must be in their grave. Hurry to the grave
to bury the curse and their cause so the burning creek
and swamp may stand still for the drilling rig, its foot
planted in the core of their earth by the ace lifter.

Hurry them down, hurry them down, the witches prescribe
sacrifice. At Ramadan, I will prove my faith
by spurning Allah's grace to slit man and ram. Hurry!
hurry! The world closes around me and I see Ken's
spirit singing, his pipe now a gun pointed at me
and I quail with a terror I cannot describe!

Hurry him down, hurry them down into the grave
time races against me swifter than the horse
and my eyes redder than the blood I have spilled
grow too heavy for my face. Hurry to the grave
before my barrel runs over with the last drop
hurry! hurry! and save me from the brave.

4 The Good Pupil

Years of steady understudy had cleared
the needed footpath through the gross thicket
of his mind. Too feeble for sums or spelling
he would excel in turning guns to crickets
to shrill wildly across the land. And biding
his time, learn through fear to be the feared.

Luckily for him, he was in the right place
where poetry, philosophy or kissing
are alien arts, where booty and the honours
of state await the unquestioning
murderer, who ponders only When and How
his act will glitter like rubies of blood and blaze
his name. One moment came gift-wrapped in the folds
of a fool's robes when his country dangled

from the web of his ex-master's plots.
He needed no speeches pressed in the false moulds
of learning and wisdom, only threats angled
to strike deepest at the wound. With frayed cloths

and blistering pepper, he would bind the gash,
raw and red, festering beneath his bayonet.
He steadied his nerves downing endless shots
of his gin-and-blood cocktail pressed from the earth
by the barrel, opening to the quick maggot
his slowed liver and the stone called his heart.

But he always had a crippling fear to staunch
so he could claim valour in the mask
of a soldier's kit. And like the school bully,
one dare with a heart proved too great a task
for his nerves. And fleeing into the valley
of bones he broke, he learnt well his lesson.